American Heart
Association®

Learn and Live sm

Family & Friends™ CPR

ISBN 0-87493-487-7

© 2006 American Heart Association

Contents

CONTENTS

Considerations for International Readers

The following table is intended for international participants of this course. It is meant to help explain information in this course that may be relevant only to those in the United States. For more specific information about your local practices and organizations please contact your instructor.

Page 4	In the section **How to Push on the Chest**, Step 5, please note the following metric conversion: 1½ to 2 inches = 4 to 5 cm
Page 37	In the section **Post Emergency Numbers,** the telephone number for the US National Poison Control Center (800-222-1222) is for the United States only. Please ask your instructor for the Poison Control number in your area.

Introduction

Program Goal	*Family & Friends™ CPR* teaches you how to give CPR to an adult, child, or infant.
Why CPR Is Important	Heart attack, drowning, electric shock, and other problems may cause a victim's heart to stop pumping blood. This is called cardiac arrest.
	Studies show that effective CPR right away improves survival from cardiac arrest. Many cardiac arrests happen outside a hospital. Most happen at home with family members. *You can make a difference,* and the first step is learning CPR.
	You may need to use the CPR skills you learn to help a family member or a friend.
Who Should Take This Program	We created this program for anyone who wants to learn CPR and does not need a course completion card in CPR.
How This Program Is Organized	You will learn CPR basics through this book and the video for the program. You will have a chance to practice many times while the video guides you. When you are not practicing with the video, you may watch the video, watch the other students practice, or follow along in your book.
Using This Book	You should use this book in the following ways:

When	Then you should
Before the program	Read this book and look at the pictures on each page.
During the program	Use this book to help you understand the important information and skills taught in the program.
After the program	Review the skills frequently. This will help you remember the steps of CPR, and you will be ready if there is an emergency.

Parts of This Book   This book has the following parts:

- Adult CPR
- Child CPR
- Adult/Child Choking
- Infant CPR
- Infant Choking
- Introduction to Automated External Defibrillators (AEDs)
- The Emergency Call

Reminders   Your book includes CPR reminders. Keep them handy to help you remember the steps of CPR.

Adult CPR

What You Will Learn	By the end of this section you should be able to give CPR to an adult.
Age for Adult CPR	Adult CPR is for victims 8 years of age and older.
Basic Steps	If you know *when* to phone your emergency response number (or 911) and *how* to push on the chest and give breaths, your actions may save a life. In this program you will learn the basic steps of CPR first. Then you will put these steps together in order. The basic steps of giving CPR are ■ Pushing on the chest ■ Giving breaths that make the chest rise
Pushing on the Chest	One of the most important parts of adult CPR is pushing on the chest. When you push on the chest, you pump blood to the brain and heart.

How to Push on the Chest

Follow these steps to push on the chest:

Step	Action
1	Kneel at the victim's side.
2	Make sure the victim is lying on his back on a firm, flat surface. If the victim is lying facedown, carefully roll him onto his back.
3	Quickly move or remove clothes from the front of the chest that will get in the way of pushing on the chest.
4	Put the heel of one hand on the center of the victim's chest between the nipples (Figure 1A). Put the heel of your other hand on top of the first hand (Figure 1B).
5	Push straight down on the chest 1½ to 2 inches with each push. Push hard and fast.
6	Repeat at a rate of 100 pushes a minute.
7	After each push, release pressure on the chest to let it come back to its normal position.

A

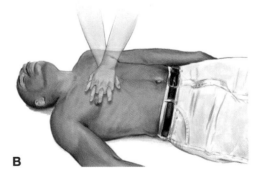

B

Figure 1. Pushing on the chest. **A,** Put the heel of one hand on the center of the chest between the nipples. **B,** Put the other hand on top of the first hand.

Open the Airway

When giving CPR, you must give the victim breaths that make the chest rise. Before giving breaths, you must open the airway by tilting the head and lifting the chin (Figure 2).

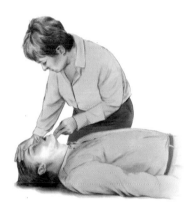

Figure 2. Open the airway by tilting the head and lifting the chin.

How to Open the Airway

Follow these steps to open the airway:

Step	Action
1	Tilt the head by pushing back on the forehead (Figure 2).
2	Lift the chin by putting your fingers on the bony part of the chin. Do not press the soft part of the neck or under the chin.
3	Lift the chin to move the jaw forward.

Giving Breaths

Your breaths give a victim air when he cannot breathe on his own.

How to Give Breaths

Follow these steps to give breaths:

Step	Action
1	Hold the airway open by tilting the head and lifting the chin (Figure 2).
2	Pinch the nose closed.
3	Take a normal breath and cover the victim's mouth with your mouth (Figure 3).
4	Give 2 breaths (blow for 1 second each). Watch for chest rise as you give each breath.

Figure 3. Give 2 breaths.

Pushes and Breaths

When you give CPR, you do sets of 30 pushes and 2 breaths. Try not to interrupt pushing on the chest for more than a few seconds. For example, don't take too long to give breaths.

Now you will learn how to give pushes and breaths in the right order.

Putting It All Together

You have learned pushes and breaths for an adult. To put it all together in the right order, follow these steps.

Make Sure the Scene Is Safe

Before you give CPR, make sure the scene is safe for you and the victim. For example, make sure there is no traffic in the area that could injure you (Figure 4). You do not want to become a victim yourself.

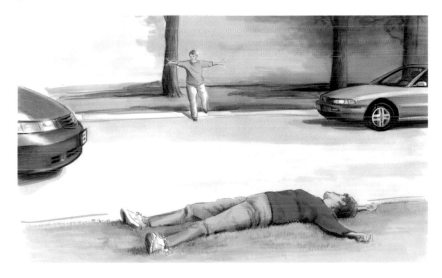

Figure 4. Make sure the scene is safe.

Check for Response

Check to see if the victim responds before giving CPR. Kneel at the victim's side. Tap the victim and shout, "Are you OK?" (Figure 5).

 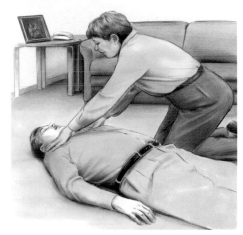

Figure 5. Check for response.

Get Help   If the victim does not respond, it is important to get help on the way as soon as possible. Follow these steps to get help:

Step	Action
1	If the victim does not respond, yell for help. If someone comes, send that person to phone your emergency response number (or 911) and get the AED (if available), which is used to shock the heart. You will learn more about AEDs later.
2	If no one comes, leave the victim to phone your emergency response number (or 911) (Figure 6) and get the AED (if available). Return to the victim and start the steps of CPR.

Figure 6. Get help. Phone your emergency response number (or 911).

Check Breathing

Once you have checked the victim for a response, you must check to see if the victim is breathing normally.

Step	Action
1	Open the victim's airway by tilting the head and lifting the chin.
2	Check to see if the victim is breathing normally (take at least 5 seconds but no more than 10 seconds) (Figure 7). • Put your ear next to the victim's mouth and nose. • **Look** to see if the chest rises. • **Listen** for breaths. • **Feel** for breaths on your cheek.

Figure 7. Look, listen, and feel for normal breathing.

Special Situations

Gasps Are Not Breaths

In the first few minutes after the heart stops, a victim may only gasp.

Gasping is *not* breathing.

Important: If the victim gasps when you open the airway to check breathing, continue the steps of CPR. The victim is likely to need all the steps of CPR.

If the First Breath Does Not Go In

If you give a victim a breath and it does not go in, you will need to re-open the airway by tilting the head and lifting the chin before giving the second breath. After you give 2 breaths, you will push on the chest 30 times. You will repeat the sets of 30 pushes and 2 breaths until the victim starts to move or trained help takes over. Trained help could be someone whose job is taking care of people who are ill or injured, such as an EMS responder, nurse, or doctor.

Side Position

If the victim is breathing normally but is not responding, roll the victim to his side and wait for trained help to take over (Figure 8). If the victim stops moving again, you will need to start the steps of CPR from the beginning.

Figure 8. Side position.

Summary of Steps for Adult CPR

The following table summarizes the steps for adult CPR.

Step	Action
1	Make sure the scene is safe.
2	Make sure the victim is lying on his back on a firm, flat surface. If the victim is lying facedown, carefully roll him onto his back.
3	Kneel at the victim's side. Tap and shout to see if the victim responds.
4	If the victim does not respond, yell for help. • If someone comes, send that person to phone your emergency response number (or 911) and get the AED (if available). • If no one comes, leave to phone your emergency response number (or 911) and get the AED (if available). After you answer all of the dispatcher's questions, return to the victim and start the steps of CPR.
5	Open the airway by tilting the head and lifting the chin.
6	Check to see if the victim is breathing normally (take at least 5 seconds but no more than 10 seconds). • Put your ear next to the victim's mouth and nose. • **Look** to see if the chest rises. • **Listen** for breaths. • **Feel** for breaths on your cheek.

Step	Action
7	If there is no normal breathing, give 2 breaths (1 second each). Watch for chest rise as you give each breath.
8	Quickly move or remove clothes from the front of the chest that will get in the way of pushing on the chest.
9	Push on the chest 30 times at a rate of 100 a minute and then give 2 breaths. After each push, release pressure on the chest to let it come back to its normal position.
10	Keep giving sets of 30 pushes and 2 breaths until the victim starts to move or trained help takes over.

Child CPR

What You Will Learn

By the end of this section you should be able to give CPR to a child.

Ages of Children

For purposes of this program, a child is 1 to 8 years of age.

Overview

While some steps for giving CPR to an adult and child are similar, there are a few differences:

- When to phone your emergency response number (or 911)
- Amount of air for breaths
- How deep to push
- How many hands for pushes

When to Phone Your Emergency Response Number (or 911)

If you are alone, do 5 sets of 30 pushes on the chest and 2 breaths *before* leaving the victim to phone your emergency response number (or 911). This is different from adult CPR, where you phone first.

Amount of Air for Breaths

Breaths are very important for children who do not respond. When giving breaths to children, be sure to open the airway and give breaths that make the chest rise, just as for adults. For small children, you will not need to use the same amount of air for breaths as for larger children or adults. However, each breath should still make the chest rise.

How Deep to Push   When you push on a child's chest, press straight down ⅓ to ½ the depth of the chest (Figure 9).

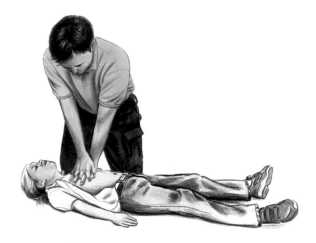

Figure 9. Two-handed compressions.

How Many Hands for Pushes   You may need to use only one hand to push on the chest of very small children (Figure 10). Whether you use one hand or 2 hands, it is important to be sure to push straight down ⅓ to ½ the depth of the chest.

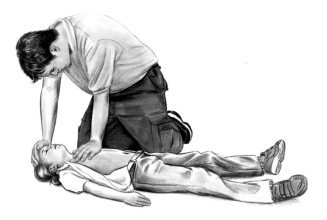

Figure 10. One-handed compressions.

Summary of Steps for Child CPR

The following table shows the steps for giving CPR to a child 1 to 8 years of age:

Step	Action
1	Make sure the scene is safe.
2	Make sure the victim is lying on her back on a firm, flat surface. If the victim is lying facedown, carefully roll her onto her back.
3	Kneel at the victim's side. Tap and shout to see if the victim responds.
4	If the victim does not respond, yell for help. • If someone comes, send that person to phone your emergency response number (or 911) and get the AED (if available). • If no one comes, stay with the child and start the steps of CPR.
5	Open the airway by tilting the head and lifting the chin.
6	Check to see if the victim is breathing (take at least 5 seconds but no more than 10 seconds). • Put your ear next to the victim's mouth and nose. • **Look** to see if the chest rises. • **Listen** for breaths. • **Feel** for breaths on your cheek.
7	If the child is not breathing, give 2 breaths (1 second each). Watch for chest rise as you give each breath.
8	Quickly move or remove clothes from the front of the chest that will get in the way of pushing on the chest.
9	Push on the chest 30 times at a rate of 100 a minute and then give 2 breaths. After each push, release pressure on the chest to let it come back to its normal position.
10	After 5 sets of 30 pushes and 2 breaths, if someone has not done this, phone your emergency response number (or 911) and get the AED (if available).
11	After you answer all of the dispatcher's questions, return to the child and start the steps of CPR.
12	Keep giving sets of 30 pushes and 2 breaths until the victim starts to move or trained help takes over.

Special Situations

When giving CPR to children 1 to 8 years of age, you handle special situations, such as re-opening the airway if the first breath does not go in and the side position, the same way as you do for adults.

Adult/Child Choking

What You Will Learn

By the end of this section you should be able to

- List the signs of choking
- Show how to help a choking victim 1 year of age and older

Signs and Actions for Choking

When food or an object like a toy gets in the airway, it can block the airway. Adults and children can easily choke while eating. Children can also easily choke when playing with small toys.

Choking can be scary. If the block in the airway is severe, you must act quickly to remove the block. If you do, you can help the victim breathe.

Use the following table to know whether a victim is choking:

If the victim	The block in the airway is	And you should
• Can make sounds • Can cough loudly	Mild	• Stand by and let her cough • If you are worried about the victim's breathing, phone your emergency response number (or 911)
• Cannot breathe • Has a cough that is very quiet or has no sound • Cannot talk or make a sound • Cannot cry (younger child) • Has high-pitched, noisy breathing • Has bluish lips or skin • Makes the choking sign	Severe	• Act quickly • Follow the steps below

---

FYI: The Choking Sign

If someone is choking, he might use the choking sign (holding the neck with one or both hands (Figure 11).

Figure 11. The choking sign. The victim holds his neck with one or both hands.

How to Help a Choking Person Over 1 Year of Age

When someone is choking and suddenly cannot breathe, talk, or make any sounds, give thrusts slightly above the belly button. These thrusts are sometimes called the Heimlich maneuver. Each thrust pushes air from the lungs like a cough. This can help remove an object blocking the airway. You should give thrusts until the object is forced out and the victim can breathe, cough, or talk or until the person stops responding.

Follow these steps to help a choking person who is 1 year of age and older:

Step	Action
1	If you think the victim is choking, ask, "Are you choking?" If he nods yes, tell him you are going to help.
2	Kneel or stand firmly behind him and wrap your arms around him so that your hands are in front.
3	Make a fist with one hand.
4	Put the thumb side of your fist slightly above his belly button and well below the breastbone.
5	Grasp the fist with your other hand and give quick up-ward thrusts into his belly (Figure 12).
6	Give thrusts until the object is forced out and he can breathe, cough, or talk or until he stops responding.

Figure 12. Helping a choking victim.

**Actions for
a Choking
Person
Who Stops
Responding**

If you cannot remove the object, the victim will stop responding.
When the victim stops responding, follow these steps:

Step	Action
1	Yell for help. If someone comes, send that person to phone your emergency response number (or 911) and get the AED (if available).
2	Lower the victim to the ground, faceup. If you are alone with an adult victim, phone your emergency response number (or 911) and get the AED (if available).
3	Return to the victim and start the steps of CPR.
4	Every time you open the airway to give breaths, open the victim's mouth wide and look for the object (Figure 13). If you see an object, remove it with your fingers. If you do not see an object, keep giving sets of 30 pushes and 2 breaths until the victim starts to move or trained help takes over.

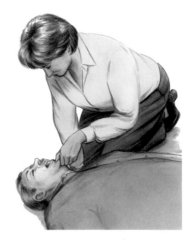

Figure 13. Open the victim's mouth wide and look for the object.

Actions to Help a Choking Large Person or Pregnant Woman

If the choking victim is in the late stages of pregnancy or is very large, give thrusts on the chest instead of thrusts on the belly (Figure 14).

Follow the same steps as above except for where you place your arms and hands. Put your arms under the victim's armpits and your hands in the center of the victim's chest. Pull straight back to give the chest thrusts.

Figure 14. Chest thrusts on a choking large person or pregnant woman.

Infant CPR

What You Will Learn	By the end of this section you should be able to give CPR to an infant.
Ages for Infant CPR	Infant CPR is for victims from birth to 1 year of age.
Pushing on the Chest	When you learn infant CPR, you will first learn each of the skills of CPR. Then you will learn to put these steps together in the correct order. The basic steps of infant CPR are ■ Pushing on the chest ■ Giving breaths that make the chest rise

How to Push on the Chest

Pushing on the chest is a very important part of infant CPR. The pushes pump blood to the brain and heart. Follow these steps to push on the chest of an infant:

Step	Action
1	Place the infant on a firm, flat surface. If possible, place the infant on a surface above the ground, such as a table. This makes it easier to give CPR to the infant.
2	Quickly move or open clothes from the front of the chest that will get in the way of pushing on the chest.
3	Put 2 fingers of one hand just below the nipple line (Figure 15). Do not put your fingers over the very bottom of the breastbone.
4	Press the infant's chest straight down ⅓ to ½ the depth of the chest. Push hard and fast.
5	Repeat at a rate of 100 pushes a minute.
6	After each push, release pressure on the chest to let it come back to its normal position.

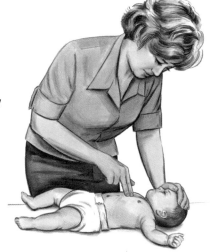

Figure 15. Put 2 fingers just below the nipple line.

Open the Airway

When giving CPR, you must give the infant breaths that make the chest rise. Before giving breaths, you must open the airway by tilting the head and lifting the chin.

How to Open the Airway

Follow these steps to open the airway:

Step	Action
1	Tilt the infant's head by pushing back on the forehead.
2	Put your fingers on the bony part of the infant's chin and lift (Figure 16). Do not press the soft part of the neck or under the chin.

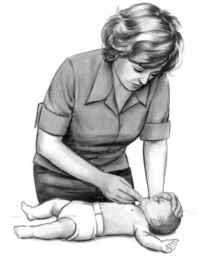

Figure 16. Open the airway by tilting the head and lifting the chin.

| Giving Breaths | Breaths are very important for infants who are not breathing or do not respond. Your breaths give an infant air when the infant cannot breathe on his own. You will not have to give as large a breath to an infant as you give to a child or an adult. |

| How to Give Breaths | Follow these steps to give breaths to an infant: |

Step	Action
1	Hold the infant's airway open by tilting the head and lifting the chin.
2	Take a normal breath. Cover the infant's mouth and nose with your mouth (Figure 17).
3	Give 2 breaths (blow for 1 second each). Watch for chest rise as you give each breath.

Figure 17. Cover the infant's mouth and nose with your mouth.

> ### FYI: Tips for Giving Breaths
> If your mouth is too small to cover the infant's mouth and nose, put your mouth over the infant's nose and give breaths through the infant's nose. (You may need to hold the infant's mouth closed to stop air from coming out through the mouth.)

| Pushes and Breaths | When doing CPR, you give sets of 30 pushes and 2 breaths. Remember to push at a rate of 100 times a minute and push hard and fast. After each push, release pressure on the chest to let it come back to its normal position. Try not to interrupt pushing on the chest for more than a few seconds. For example, don't take too long to give breaths.

Now you will learn how to give pushes and breaths in the right order. |

Putting It All Together	You have learned pushes and breaths for an infant. To put it all together in the right order, follow these steps.
Make Sure the Scene Is Safe	Before you give CPR, make sure the scene is safe for you and the victim. For example, make sure there are no downed electrical lines in the area. You do not want to become a victim yourself.
Check for Response	Check to see if the infant responds before giving CPR. Tap the infant's foot and shout, "Are you OK?" (Figure 18).

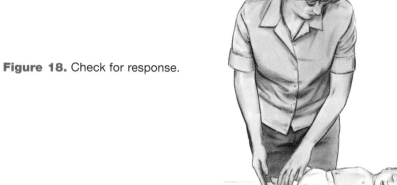

Figure 18. Check for response.

Get Help	If the infant does not respond, it is important to get help on the way as soon as possible. Follow these steps to get help:

Step	Action
1	If the infant does not respond, yell for help. If someone comes, send that person to phone your emergency response number (or 911).
2	If no one comes, stay with the infant and continue the steps of CPR.

Check Breathing

Once you have checked the infant for a response, you must check to see if the infant is breathing.

Step	Action
1	Open the infant's airway by tilting the head and lifting the chin.
2	Check to see if the infant is breathing (take at least 5 seconds but no more than 10 seconds) (Figure 19). • Put your ear next to the infant's mouth and nose. • **Look** to see if the chest rises. • **Listen** for breaths. • **Feel** for breaths on your cheek.

Figure 19. Look, listen, and feel for breaths.

Special Situation

If you give an infant a breath and it does not go in, you will need to re-open the airway by tilting the head and lifting the chin before giving the second breath.

Summary of Steps for Infant CPR

The following table summarizes the steps for infant CPR:

Step	Action
1	Make sure the scene is safe.
2	Tap the infant's foot and shout to see if the infant responds.
3	If the infant does not respond, yell for help. • If someone comes, send that person to phone your emergency response number (or 911). • If no one comes, stay with the infant and continue the steps of CPR.

Step	Action
4	Place the infant on a firm, flat surface. If possible, place the infant on a surface above the ground, such as a table.
5	Open the airway by tilting the head and lifting the chin.
6	Check to see if the infant is breathing (take at least 5 seconds but no more than 10 seconds). • Put your ear next to the infant's mouth and nose. • **Look** to see if the chest rises. • **Listen** for breaths. • **Feel** for breaths on your cheek.
7	If the infant is not breathing, give 2 breaths (1 second each). Watch for chest rise as you give each breath.
8	Quickly move or open clothes from the front of the chest that will get in the way of pushing on the chest.
9	Push on the chest 30 times at a rate of 100 a minute and then give 2 breaths. After each push, release pressure on the chest to let it come back to its normal position.
10	After 5 sets of 30 pushes and 2 breaths, if someone has not done this, phone your emergency response number (or 911).
11	After you answer all of the dispatcher's questions, return to the infant and start the steps of CPR.
12	Keep giving sets of 30 pushes and 2 breaths until the infant starts to move or trained help takes over.

FYI: Taking the Infant With You to Phone for Help

If the infant is not injured and you are alone, after 5 sets of 30 pushes and 2 breaths, you may carry the infant with you to phone your emergency response number (or 911).

Infant Choking

What You Will Learn

By the end of this section you should be able to

- List the signs of choking
- Show how to help a choking infant

Signs of Choking

When food or an object like a toy gets in the airway, it can block the airway. Infants can easily choke if they put small things in their mouths.

Choking can be scary. If the block in the airway is severe, you must act to remove the block. If you act quickly, you can help the victim breathe.

Use the table below to know if a victim is choking:

If the victim	The block in the airway is	And you should
• Can make sounds • Can cough loudly	Mild	• Stand by and let the infant cough • If you are worried about the infant's breathing, *phone your emergency response number (or 911)*
• Cannot breathe • Has a cough that is very quiet or has no sound • Cannot make a sound or cry • Has high-pitched, noisy breathing • Has bluish lips or skin	Severe	• Act quickly • Follow the steps below

How to Help a Choking Infant

When an infant is choking and suddenly cannot breathe or make any sounds, you must act quickly to help get the object out by using back slaps and chest thrusts.

Follow these steps to help a choking infant:

Step	Action
1	Hold the infant facedown on your forearm. Support the infant's head and jaw with your hand. Sit or kneel and rest your arm on your lap or thigh.
2	Give up to 5 back slaps with the heel of your free hand between the infant's shoulder blades (Figure 20).
3	If the object does not come out after 5 back slaps, turn the infant onto his back. Move or open the clothes from the front of the infant's chest only if you can do so quickly. You can push on the chest through clothes if you need to.
4	Give up to 5 chest thrusts using 2 fingers of your free hand to push on the chest in the same place you push during CPR (Figure 21). • Support the head and neck. • Hold the infant with one hand and arm, resting your arm on your lap or thigh.
5	Repeat giving 5 back slaps and 5 chest thrusts until the object comes out and the infant can breathe, cough, or cry or until the infant stops responding.

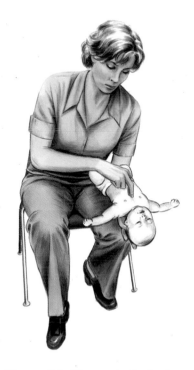

Figure 20. Give up to 5 back slaps with the heel of your hand.

Figure 21. Give up to 5 chest thrusts.

When to Stop Back Slaps and Chest Thrusts

Stop back slaps and chest thrusts if

- The object comes out
- The infant begins to breathe, cough, or cry
- The infant stops responding

Actions for a Choking Infant Who Stops Responding

If you cannot remove the object, the infant will stop responding. When the infant stops responding, follow these steps:

Step	Action
1	Yell for help. If someone comes, send that person to phone your emergency response number (or 911). Stay with the infant to start the steps of CPR.
2	Place the infant on a firm, flat surface. If possible, place the infant on a surface above the ground, such as a table.
3	Continue the steps of CPR.
4	Every time you open the airway to give breaths, open the infant's mouth wide and look for the object. If you see an object, remove it with your fingers. If you do not see an object, keep giving sets of 30 pushes and 2 breaths. Continue CPR until the infant starts to move or trained help takes over.

Do Not
DO NOT give thrusts on an infant's belly because this could injure an infant.

Introduction to Automated External Defibrillators (AEDs)

What You Will Learn

By the end of this section you should be able to tell what an AED does.

Overview

The automated external defibrillator (AED) is a machine with a computer inside (Figure 22). An AED can

- Recognize some heart problems that require a shock
- Tell the rescuer when a shock is needed
- Give a shock if needed

AEDs are accurate and easy to use. After very little training, most people can use an AED. If you start CPR right away and use an AED within a few minutes, you will have the best chance of saving the life of someone whose heart has stopped.

Figure 22. An automated external defibrillator (AED).

Steps for Using an AED

There are 4 simple steps for using an AED:

Step	Action
1	Turn the AED on. Follow the prompts you see and hear.
2	Attach the pads.
3	Let the AED check the victim's heart rhythm.
4	Push the shock button if the AED tells you to do so.

If you would like to take a class on how to use an AED, visit *www.americanheart.org/cpr* or call 877-AHA-4CPR (877-242-4277) to find a class near you.

The Emergency Call

What You Will Learn

By the end of this section you should be able to

- Tell how to phone your emergency response number (or 911)
- Tell how to answer a dispatcher's questions

Post Emergency Numbers

At times you will need to phone your emergency response number (or 911) for help. Keep emergency numbers near or on the telephone(s), including your emergency response number and Poison Control (800-222-1222)

> ***Your Emergency Response Number***
> My emergency response number is _____
> (fill in the blank).

Reasons to Phone for Help

Many times the emergency response number is 911. As a general rule, you should phone your emergency response number and ask for help whenever

- Someone is seriously ill or hurt
- You are not sure what to do in an emergency

Remember: It is better to phone for help even if you might not need it than not to phone when someone does need help.

Answering Dispatcher Questions

When you phone your emergency response number (or 911), the dispatcher will ask you some questions about the emergency. You need to stay on the phone until the dispatcher tells you to hang up. The dispatcher can also tell you how to help the victim until trained help takes over.

Conclusion

Congratulations on taking time to attend this program. Contact the American Heart Association if you want more information on CPR, AEDs, or even first aid. You can visit *www.americanheart.org/cpr* or call 877-AHA-4CPR (877-242-4277) to find a class near you.

Even if you don't remember all the steps of CPR exactly, it is important for you to try. And always remember to phone your emergency response number (or 911). They can remind you what to do.